ON LOUGH DERG

WORDS BY DEIRDRE PURCELL

"ON LOUGH DERG"

PHOTOGRAPHS BY LIAM BLAKE

COMMENTARY BY
BISHOP JOSEPH DUFFY D.D.

First published 1988 by
Veritas Publications
7/8 Lower Abbey Street
Dublin 1
Ireland

British Library Cataloguing in Publication Data

Purcell, Deirdre
    On Lough Derg
    1. (County) Donegal. Lough Derg. Visitors' guides
    I. Title
    914.19'304824

    ISBN 1-85390-012-5

Produced by Town House
41 Marlborough Road
Donnybrook
Dublin 4

Design by Bill Murphy, MSIA, MSDI
Typeset by Printset & Design Ltd, Dublin
Colour reproduction by Kulor Centre
Printed in Ireland by Criterion Press Ltd

LOUGH DERG

PART 1

COMMENTARY BY
BISHOP JOSEPH DUFFY D.D.

LOUGH DERG

Lough Derg is a remote, rocky island in a mountain lake in County Donegal in Ireland. It is by normal standards an off-putting place: wind-swept and desolate; often bitterly cold and wet; at other times unbearably clammy and hot. The nearest village is five miles away; the nearest town over twenty. The access road is narrow and twisty. The landscape is barren and mountainy. Even the mountains are low and unspectacular. Yet every year during the summer months, between twenty and thirty thousand people come here to spend three days in prayer and penance, of a kind unknown elsewhere in the Christian world.

Why do they come, these thousands of men and women, old and young, from town and country, from every walk and station of life?

It must be said that Lough Derg is not easily understood by observers who are not pilgrims. The journalist or historian or tourist as such will not have a rewarding time in this extraordinary place. The level of conversation may be interesting at times; but one can think of more convivial and certainly more comfortable meeting places to find out what people are saying and thinking. The historian will get plenty of reminiscence from older pilgrims but will soon discover here an indistinguishable mixture of fact and fancy which has been a special feature of Lough Derg since earliest times. The tourist will be equally disappointed. There is little to see that is memorable or even different, apart from a number of ruins of monastic beehive cells, a splendid new hostel, and an elegant church from the 1920s.

Why then do they come? Because this is no ordinary place. Because Lough Derg has a secret which it reveals only to the believing pilgrim. It is a secret which transforms this inhospitable rock into a haven of peace, a secret which removes the barriers of sin and fear, of ill-fortune and misery. A medieval Gaelic poet wrote of his pilgrimage:

> *My heart of stony hardness, my eye as unfeeling as my heart, my mouth of guileful speech — all these have I quelled in penance.*

For all that, the secret of Lough Derg is elusive, as mysterious as the gift of religious faith which makes it possible. Another bardic poet came to Lough Derg and left as he came, without the spiritual lift he had hoped for:

> *O Son of God, Creator of all, who shunned not the death of the three nails, I am ashamed for this pilgrimage to Lough Derg with my heart as hard as stone.*

What is most tangible and totally predictable on Lough Derg on the other hand is the struggle which awaits the pilgrim.

PILGRIMAGE IN THE CHRISTIAN TRADITION

In order to appreciate why people come to such a place, it is necessary to understand the nature of pilgrimage. Pilgrims who take the bus from Dublin to Lough Derg, or who set out by car from West Cork or Kilkenny, are performing a religious exercise which is as old as the first book of the Old Testament. The first biblical pilgrimage is recorded in Genesis, chapter 35, when Jacob was told to go to Bethel because it was there that God had originally appeared to him. In the time of Christ the great centre of pilgrimage was Jerusalem. The first Christians continued to make the sacred journey there for the great feasts. Later, when the centuries of persecution ended for Christians, they began to visit the holy places in large numbers, places where the Lord and his followers had walked. This movement was interrupted by the Muslim conquest of Palestine, but received new impetus in the time of the Crusades, whose main purpose was to free the way to Jerusalem for the pilgrims of the day. Next to Jerusalem, the most honoured spot in the Christian world was Rome, where the apostles Peter and Paul had found 'the place of their resurrection'. All Catholic bishops to this day make a five-yearly pilgrimage *ad limina apostolorum* (to the tombs of the apostles). The third most important place of pilgrimage in medieval times was the shrine of St James of Compostella in the north-west of Spain. We read, for example, of one Maguire chieftain of Fermanagh who made at least two visits there in the fifteenth century.

During this period, almost every country in western Europe developed its own special 'holy place'. There was Canterbury in England, Bruges in Belgium, Tours in France, Aachen and Cologne in Germany and Loreto in Italy. It was also at this time, certainly from the twelfth century, that pilgrims began to make their way to St Patrick's Purgatory on Lough Derg in Ireland. By 1492 its importance was such that it was the only Irish site marked on a map of the world in that year.

Medieval scholars today are attaching more and more significance to this great pilgrimage movement throughout Europe. It was, it seems, a major influence in bringing people together and in helping to form the common Christian culture which characterised medieval Europe. Only a few years ago a large fresco was discovered in a convent in the small Italian town of Todi which shows that Lough Derg was known there in the middle of the fourteenth century. It is obviously a matter of pride for today's pilgrims that Lough Derg was in the mainstream of this great movement. Scholars are taking a renewed interest in the medieval accounts of pilgrims from France, Hungary, Spain, England and Holland, all of whom came to Ireland in search of the spiritual experience promised by a visit to Lough Derg.

PLACE OF SANCTUARY AND RETREAT

The only access road to Lough Derg is from the village of Pettigo. Pettigo is a quiet crossroads sitting on the border between the Republic of Ireland and Northern Ireland. The border road running out of the village to the east stretches into the lowlands of Fermanagh, along the northern shore of Lough Erne and makes its way to Enniskillen and the north and east of Ireland. This is the route of the Dublin bus which gives a daily service throughout the pilgrimage season. The other road out of Pettigo goes westwards into the hill country towards Donegal town and southwards to Sligo and the west of Ireland.

Nowadays, the pilgrims travel to Lough Derg by coach and car. Until the closure of the Great Northern Railway in 1957, the popular mode of transport was the train, notably the Bundoran Express, which came all the way from Dublin and Dundalk. Until the bus became common, the journey from Pettigo to the shore of the island was made by jaunting-car. Before the advent of public transport many pilgrims travelled on foot and made their way over the hills on recognised pilgrim routes. In 1727 pilgrims carried a staff and approached the island as follows:

> As soon as the pilgrims come within sight of the Holy Island, they pull off their shoes and stockings and uncover their heads and walk thus with their beads in one hand and sometimes a cross in the other, to the lakeside, from whence they are wafted over, paying each one sixpence for their freight.

The pilgrim today only observes one rule before arriving on the island, that of fasting from the previous midnight. It is this fast which turns the journey into a pilgrimage, which links pilgrims with each other and with all those who have come here over the centuries in search of God.

Pettigo, the gateway to Lough Derg, derives its name from the Latin *protectio*, a word which means 'protected land' or 'sanctuary'. The Irish equivalent is *tearmann,* which occurs frequently in placenames. In fact the whole area surrounding Lough Derg was known in ancient times as Termon Davog. Davog, one of the great monastic saints of Ireland, was the earliest saint associated with Lough Derg. The tradition in the seventeenth century was that he came from Wales as a disciple of St Patrick and that he founded a monastery and a penitential retreat on Lough Derg where Patrick had experienced a vision of the pains of purgatory. The monastery was on a large island known as Saints' Island and was quite distinct from the place of penitential retreat which was, and still is, on the smaller island known as Station Island. It is to this island that today's pilgrims come. By the eleventh century the property of the monastery had extended as far as Pettigo and the surrounding countryside and the area became known as Termon Davog. In due course the cult of Davog spread further afield, over the whole of Donegal and West Tyrone.

Davog's monastery on Saints' Island was the beginning of Christianity in the area. It was his monks who set up the cells or oratories, which are now known as 'beds', on the pilgrimage island, places away from the community where the monks could cultivate quiet prayer.

The idea of a place of retreat was prominent in the Celtic monastic system. It catered for the small number of monks in the typical monastery who wished to lead an ascetic life. For the lay person, it meant leaving a comfortable home. The following is an extract from a tenth-century, Irish poem. The world today may be different from that of the tenth century but the reasons for making a penitential retreat remain the same. Here the poet asks the perennial questions:

> *Shall I go, O King of the Mysteries, after my fill of cushions*
>   *and music,*
> *without heady drink that intoxicates,*
> *without soft clothes that are pleasant to look at,*
> *without luxuries that are no friend of any saint?*
>
> *Shall I say a long farewell to my homestead?*
> *Shall I offer myself under Christ's yoke?*
> *Shall I make my confession, swiftly and simply, on this hard*
>   *occasion?*

Lough Derg gets us away from status symbols, from the market place, from buying and selling. Fasting from food and being deprived of creature comforts make us realise how dependent we become on these things and how few of them are really necessary. Putting ourselves under a discipline which is not of our own making and which is uniform for all pilgrims is often an upheaval which forces us to rethink the priorities in our lives. It provides us with a framework to examine our attitude to success and happiness.

PURGATORY: A DRAMA IN THREE ACTS

It was by the name of 'purgatory' that Lough Derg was known in medieval times. We are told that Lough Derg helped, more than any other place, to impress the Catholic doctrine of purgatory on the popular mind and imagination.

About the twelfth century, the name purgatory came to be used to describe a third place belonging to the 'other' world, a kind of half-way house between heaven and hell. The souls who went there were assured of eternal salvation but had to undergo a cleansing punishment for their sins before they could enjoy the happiness of heaven. They could also be helped by the prayers and sacrifices of the faithful here on earth. The medievals, with their primitive notions of geography, felt that this place was somewhere in the bowels of the earth, though obviously not as remote or as terrifying as hell. They eventually pinpointed its location in a cave on a small island in a mountain lake in the north-west of Ireland.

The idea of purgatory was in total harmony with the very rigorous, ascetic practices handed down by the early Celtic monks in the period immediately after St Patrick. The first of these practices, observed by the Lough Derg pilgrim today, is a total fast from food for three days, except for one spartan meal of black tea or coffee and dry bread per day. The fast is a prayer of the body, an acknowledgement of human poverty and need in the presence of the ultimate mysteries of life, an act of solidarity with those who are dying of hunger in the world. By feeling a little hunger ourselves we become more conscious of their cry for help.

The second act of this drama is a prolonged series of oral prayers, recited while walking around the penitential 'beds'.

While making these prayers, the pilgrims walk barefoot over rough stones and rocks. Like the fast it is initially a physical exercise but opens up spiritual possibilities in keeping with the rest of the programme. The mental effort to negotiate sharp stones while counting prayers has a relaxing effect, especially in the open air. The more one gets absorbed, the less overpowered one feels by cares and worries, the less disturbed by the weight of the world. The form and content of the prayer cease to matter as long as they become a forward movement toward one's goal.

Act three is a full twenty-four-hour vigil, begun only when the pilgrim has already completed a day's fast and three rounds of the penitential beds. The vigil is the heart of the entire pilgrimage and from the physical point of view is by far the most difficult. Unlike the other acts, the fast and the beds, it is a group exercise, where prayers are recited in unison and where pilgrims help one another by their encouragement and example to keep awake through the long night and still longer day. The vigil concentrates the mind as well as the body. The emphasis is more on time than on movement. There is no rush, no coming and going in a hurry, no being late or even arriving at the last minute. When prayers are over there is nothing to do except take the fresh air and engage in conversation in order to keep awake.

Medieval accounts of the Lough Derg pilgrimage concentrate heavily on the vigil experience. The fact that pilgrims frequently fell asleep and had very vivid dreams gave rise to a wealth of tales about the 'other' world which appealed greatly to the medieval storyteller. Because the vigil took place in a small stone cave and the pilgrim was expected to remain there for the duration, it was regarded as the ordeal *par excellence*. The pilgrim was allowed to undertake the vigil only when he had the express permission of the bishop and had listened to the advice of the prior who did his best to dissuade him. One pilgrim in the fifteenth century spent five hours in the cave before the prior came and found him senseless and out of breath. Another spent from two to three; but the norm was always the full twenty-four hours.

The cave was designed to resemble a vaulted tomb and this was a key symbol in understanding the purpose of the vigil. The liturgy included a procession with candles and a final blessing reminiscent of the funeral rite. In the eighteenth century the symbolism of death was taken to the point where a requiem Mass was celebrated for pilgrims before they went on vigil in the cave. For pilgrims today, the night on vigil is like being in a twilight zone, a form of life with gradually reduced energy and awareness. The morning air eventually helps to remove the gloom of darkness and the shadows of the night. But for the pilgrim struggling to stay awake, there is no relief from weakness and tedium. The all-night vigil continues throughout the day and the hours pass slowly.

Perhaps here we touch on the deepest meaning of Lough Derg.

The vigil experience is a parable of all human life on this earth, of life which is inescapably linked with death, and which is always a pale reflection of a life to come.

The three days spent here are in many ways a prolonged meditation on the three days of Holy Week, on the mysteries of the passion, death and resurrection of Our Saviour. Lough Derg is the story of those days translated into the lives of the thousands of men and women who come here, giving meaning and purpose to suffering and loss. Whatever the experience of individual pilgrims, the message of the pilgrimage, like the message of the Christian gospel, speaks of hope and gives solid grounds for hope in our troubled world.

ST PATRICK'S BASILICA

The link with St Patrick seems to coincide with the establishment of the Canons Regular of St Augustine on Saints' Island about the year 1130. The Canons were part of the great twelfth-century reform which affected the entire Church and which was spearheaded in Ireland by St Malachy. They remained in charge of the pilgrimage for some 500 years until their monastery was vandalised by Puritan fanatics in 1632.

St Patrick features prominently in all of the Gaelic poems on Lough Derg before the Protestant Reformation. For one poet he is the great healer, the surgeon who still binds the wounds of the Irish. For another he is the very powerful advocate who

will help those, like the poet, who are desperately in need. In recent times the *Confession of St Patrick* is vigorously promoted as the spiritual commentary which best sums up the ethos of the pilgrimage:

> *When I had come to Ireland I used to pray many times during the day. More and more my love of God and reverence for him began to increase. My faith grew stronger and my zeal so intense that in the course of a single day I would say as many as a hundred prayers, and almost as many in the night. This I did even when I was in the woods and on the mountains. Even in times of snow or frost or rain I would rise before dawn to pray. I never felt the worse for it; nor was I in any way lazy because, as I now realise, I was full of enthusiasm.*

When the practice of keeping vigil in a stone cave began, the cave was ascribed to St Patrick. In time, the association of Patrick with purgatory found its way into the works of Dante and Shakespeare and has survived to this day in the official name of Station Island: St Patrick's Purgatory. The cave seems to have been a modest affair, holding only a handful of pilgrims at any time. It survived until 1780 when it was finally closed by the Bishop of Clogher and replaced by a small chapel, called St Patrick's and sometimes the 'Prison' chapel. This chapel was in turn replaced by the present church which was given the status of a basilica by Pope Pius XI in 1931.

The basilica was designed by Professor William A Scott in 1919, having been conceived in the space of a day and a night spent on Station Island during the penitential season of that year. When Scott died in 1921 the work was continued by T J Cullen. He preserved Scott's plan of a neo-Romanesque octagon rising to a pointed copper dome, with short cruciform arms, flanking circular towers to the entrance portal, and primitive Norman arcades outside.

Scott was the inspired, almost inevitable choice of architect. He had close personal links with the Celtic revival at the turn of the century and was therefore in a unique position to express on Lough Derg the spirit of national renewal which drew inspiration from pre-Norman Irish history. His father had been a member of the Royal Society of Antiquaries of Ireland and had worked on historic buildings. Another influence on his work was a period spent in Italy and in Constantinople making a study of Byzantine basilicas. Following his earlier work the playwright and Celtic revivalist Edward Martyn said of him that "he had invented something like a modern Irish architecture inspired by old Irish buildings". He was sparing of decoration and went for a simple, austere effect, reminiscent of primitive Irish churches of the monastic period.

The basilica expresses accurately the extraordinary revival and spirit of the Lough Derg pilgrimage in the present century. It became an intensely Irish institution and was part of the revival of Irish nationalism which eventually effected political changes. The revival can be dated from the appointment of Patrick Keown as prior or priest-in-charge in 1909. Monsignor Keown was responsible for the planning and completion of the basilica which was opened in 1931. During these years Lough Derg became a truly national pilgrimage with pilgrims coming in large numbers from all over Ireland, rather than from the counties in the vicinity.

RENEWAL IN OUR TIME

The Lough Derg pilgrimage then is an elaborate, highly structured and very demanding programme of spiritual exercises. The fasting and keeping watch are solidly based in the Bible. The ritual of oral prayers repeated while walking is more a feature of Irish monastic life, especially, it would appear, on islands with religious community associations like Tory off the north Donegal coast and Inishmurray off the coast of Sligo.

There is a firm insistence on rubrical tradition in the performance of the exercises. Nothing in the programme ever changes except in minor details and for very practical reasons. The conviction is that any substantial change would destroy the pilgrimage, something which all the persecutions and privations of the past have failed to do.

Pilgrims who are aware of the programme before they come, certainly those who come back for a second time, appreciate the need for a balanced view of the Catholic Church's teaching on penance and true sorrow for sin. The idea one hears at times of making a bargain with God, as one would with an equal partner, betrays a notion of God which is unacceptable in the Christian scheme of things. It also fails to provide the motivation which is a necessary support for the pilgrim. The struggle to cope with the physical demands of Lough Derg must be accompanied by an acceptance of the deeper conflict in every believer between body and soul, between natural human instinct and Christian conscience. The serenity of mind, the message of hope and trust in the ultimate goodness of God, the purging of guilt and fear; all of these fruits of Lough Derg are in the end gratuitous and are never in the strict sense earned as of right.

A frank admission of one's own limitations must extend to the failure of the Church to bring about reconciliation in society. This presupposes that pilgrims see themselves as members of the Church and not merely as a collection of individuals who happen to belong to the same Church. It also means taking responsibility for the claims and activities of the Church, especially where these are rejected or misunderstood or simply ignored. Sensitive concern for the work of the Church as a reconciling agent in society is an area which calls for witness on Lough Derg.

15

COMMUNAL CELEBRATION

In recent years the liturgy on Lough Derg has reflected a keener sense of belonging to the Church as a community. The celebration of the Eucharist on the evening of the first day brings all the pilgrims together for the first time. The formal greeting at the beginning invites the pilgrims to see themselves as a community of believers and to strive for that greater community we call the kingdom of God. While this is a feature of every Mass, it is seldom so thoroughly prepared for as on the evening of the first day on Lough Derg.

The sacrament of reconciliation, celebrated on the morning of the second day, has always been the high point of the pilgrimage. This has been prepared for, not merely by the travelling and prayers of the first day, but by the all-night vigil and by the prayers said in common during the night. The vigil is a resolve to be alert and ready for the coming of Christ. It is also a prayer of solidarity with all who struggle in the darkness of isolation and alienation. In the morning we celebrate the forgiveness we have so earnestly sought.

The Eucharist on the morning of the third day has all the joy and excitement of the Resurrection. There is a new life and warmth in our respect for each other, brought about through our sharing in the exercises, followed by a good night's sleep. There is in this Eucharist a deeper sense than usual of giving thanks, which sends us on our way from Lough Derg the happier for having come.

LOUGH DERG

PART 2

ORDER OF EXERCISES

WORDS BY DEIRDRE PURCELL

1. *Alone in my little oratory without a single human being in my company; dear to me would such a pilgrimage be before going to meet death.*

A hidden secret little hut for the forgiveness of every fault; a conscience upright and untroubled intent on holy heaven.

Let the place which shelters me amid monastic enclosures be a beautiful spot hallowed by old stones and I all alone therein . . .

Poem, translated from the Irish,
thought to be from the eighth or ninth century.

2. *..it is a road you travel on your own...*

Seamus Heaney ('Station Island')

3. *"Although you are always surrounded by people here in Lough Derg, you can be as solitary as you like. Sometimes it is the loneliest place on earth."*

Monsignor Gerard McSorley, prior of Lough Derg

First Day
12.00 Midnight — Begin fast.

Forty-two people board the bus, thirty-nine women and girls, two men and a boy.

Most are in pairs or threesomes. They place bundles and bags on the overhead racks — ''you can never have too many clothes can you?'' — no ice to be broken, all in the same boat, or bus, all going on pilgrimage.

''Why are you doing it?''
''Well, we've just done our finals.''
''Us too.''

''I couldn't put it off any longer. It's a long-standing promise...''

''I promised I'd go last year and I can't rest this year until I go.''

Then the sorting out of counties and relationships up and down the bus.
Did you go to school in ...?
Would you be a sister of...?
I think I know your father...
I have you now! God, it's a small world!

The bus moves off seven minutes late, one insulated community drawing away from another.

It lumbers past the whiskey bonders and the tobacconists, the newsagents and the Macushla Bingo Hall, the shop selling *Groceries Fruit Veg and Fuels*, the boy eating ice-cream outside the bookies. Past tenement houses with boarded-up windows and dank deserted playgrounds, past flower stalls and female hair-palaces. A mangy white cat stalks the footpath outside Mahon Motor Factors on the North Circular Road.

Past Nash's Interior Fabrics and the Mater Hospital and Doyle's Corner and the neat front gardens of Cabra — and further out the little businesses, upholstery workshops, bockety 'For Sale' signs on small houses, a car with a canoe on its roof, men on ladders putting in replacement windows, women gossiping at the stoops.

A Tyre Exchange, a Toyota Dealer, a local Grill. A sad child leaning against a corner, an old man showing his broken ankle to a neighbour.

The pilgrims are on their own.

The sun comes out and streaks the grimy windows of the bus. "I hope it stays sunny," says a pilgrim woman to her friend. "It never does," says the pilgrim's friend, whose nineteenth pilgrimage this is.

A pilgrim woman, a woman who has plainly suffered, says with satisfaction and even triumph that Lough Derg is the Great Leveller. "We're all the one there," she says, "none of us is any better than anyone else."

Another offers propitiation: "We're all going the one place anyway." She does not mean Lough Derg.

Clonee, Navan, Cavan, Clones, across the border to the north of Ireland where the soldier at the crossing smiles indulgently and taps a Michael Jackson drumbeat on his rifle. Lisnaskea and Lisbellaw, the pilgrim bus is silent now inside. Past the flying Union Jacks (it is the Glorious Twalfth.) Enniskillen, the RUC, cynical but respectful, blocks the road to Kesh, the parades, the bands, the Union Jacks, the Lambeg Drums. The Lough Derg pilgrimage is diverted round the Williamites to Ederny and comes to Pettigo in the rain.

It rumbles through that border-rifted town, where bridgeless fifty years ago, the pilgrim hired a strong-man when the river was in flood.

The common impulse in the silent bus is to butt against this coming battle. Repeaters swore the last time they would not fight again. Novices feel the hollow pull of dread.

And then the apparition hung on sky and water, stone mirage, excalibur, riding the fearsome lake as if voided from its depths, grey on black against grey sky. Grey buildings, grey horizon, grey boats, ferry-beetles on their backs, crawling low along the glassy water, laden, heavy, always busy with moving souls.

Pilgrims arrive as early as possible (any day from 1 June to 13 August), register and await boat.

Grey tokens, little tickets from a little window. Name only, entered in a notebook. No townland, rank nor station. (*We're all the same here.*) Fresh young boatmen with applecheeks and towels for collars, solicitous at the jetty, handing down the pilgrims; older boatman, boatman man and boy, spruce in collar and tie. Cheery, jocular boatman, ferryman to Purgatory. Mr Snow.

Look ahead on landing: this purgatory has a postal service and a bright green pillar box.

Follow the stream of pilgrim women hurrying to remove their shoes.

Look right from the stream: under the tree, the sycamore, that little hill is moving, frightful splayshapes, stumbling humps... look again, the hill is human, hydraheaded, separating and congealing, hundred-armed and legged.

These are barefoot pilgrims on the penitential beds.

Look up: grey roofline pierced with many crosses, a roostered weathervane, a fish, a little boat with many oarsmen.

24

At Reception, little bed-ticket, black on blue, Cubicle 221 Bed A.

The dormitories are shining, squared off, gleaming hardwood doors and bunk beds tidy. A single hook for clothes and shelf for shoes, a basin with cold water from the lake. Bed A forbidden on this First Day, tonight it will be occupied by pilgrim of the Second Day. Tonight, the First Day pilgrims do not sleep.

And then outside, the First Day shock of wet and freezing flagstones on soles of feet grown soft.

Grey spiny buildings, the stony heart of the Beds. No softness on this island, no flower nor any bush nor tree, except the ancient dripping sycamore above the penitential beds and its seedling which was planted near the jetty. Around the Beds, beyond the reach of weary feet, a few weeds straggle for light between the stones. There is some grass, but it is rarely trodden. The feet are here for punishment.

The hundreds here are always moving, the few who sit or stand accentuate the busyness, they smoke together or alone, or sit and stare, their voices contrapuntal to the quiet.

11.00 am — Begin Stations and complete three before 9.20 pm.

Order of Station

Begin the Station with a visit to the Blessed Sacrament in St Patrick's Basilica.

There is beauty here, in clear white candle of the vigil, cool white curve of altar furniture, jewelled glowing windowglass of Harry Clarke.

Then go to St Patrick's Cross, near the Basilica; kneel, and say one *Our Father*, one *Hail Mary* and one *Creed*. Kiss the Cross.

The cross is rusted iron set on remnants of a small fluted column. Pilgrims kneel in pools of rainwater and rest their heads against the fluting, their dangling rosaries clicking softly in the gusting wind. They rise and press their lips to the rusted iron.

Go to St Brigid's Cross, on the outside wall of the Basilica; kneel, and say three *Our Fathers*, three *Hail Marys* and one *Creed*. Stand with your back to the Cross, and, with arms outstretched, renounce three times the World, the Flesh and the Devil.

The pilgrims kneel again on flooded flagstones and queue in patient silence for St Brigid's Cross. Then, eyes on stony end of hostel, three times crucify themselves against the wall, lips moving in renunciation.

Walk slowly, by your right hand, four times around the Basilica, while praying *silently* seven decades of the Rosary and one *Creed* at the end.

This is the easy part, if any part is easy. Round and round, the lake on three sides, flagstones cold but flat, puddles warmer, passing slower swishing oilskins and noisy plastic macs, sounds of gulls from across the water.

Hail Marys mounting soothingly...

Go to the penitential cell or "bed" called St Brigid's Bed (the one nearest to the bell-tower) but if there is a queue take care to join it before going to the Bed.

The pilgrims queue by fives in phalanx, stoic in the sheeting rain and wind, tasting drops from hoods and noses (the queue is sometimes for an hour or more).

Eyes are fixed on those already stumbling on the upper Beds.

The queue is quiet, but sometimes chatting to the trainee priests and seminarians who volunteer to keep the queue in order and to keep the circles moving on the Beds.

"How many were there here last weekend, Father?"

And when the answer is that numbers were upwards of twelve hundred, they nod with satisfaction that those queues were longer, far, than this.

They turn to one another: "There's something in it all the same. The numbers wouldn't be so great if there wasn't something in it..."

At the Bed
a) walk three times around the outside, by your right
hand, while saying three *Our Fathers*, **three** *Hail Marys*
and one *Creed*;
b) kneel at the entrance to the Bed and repeat these
prayers;
c) walk three times around the inside and say these
prayers again;
d) kneel at the Cross in the centre and say these prayers
for the fourth time.

The word 'walk' is a piece of black humour in the leaflet entitled 'THE PILGRIMAGE EXERCISES' by which all pilgrims regulate their days on Lough Derg. (To walk: to stroll, to stride, to ramble, to peregrinate, to promenade, to perambulate, to saunter...)

St Brigid's Bed, on the crest of the moving human hill, is a collection of asymmetrical striated rocks, slick with rain and natural oils of feet. The rocks are fractured and raised in fragments and in little troughs, so few can give security of foothold. 'Walking' on these upper Beds is a matter less of feet than of eyes and balance, searching out a ridge which fits under a curled foot-arch or which can be gripped by spread toes; reaching flailing hands to willing helpers.

A bent old man helps a thin arthritic woman.

A travelling woman wearing woollen, footless, gaily-patterned stockings, helps a tired priest with noble forehead and badly bunioned feet.

The *Hail Marys* become automatic, mantra-like.

Priest that evening at the Holy Hour: "When your lips are fully occupied and so is your body, there can be stillness in your heart..."

Repeat these exercises at
St Brendan's Bed,
St Catherine's Bed,
St Columba's Bed.

Rain bucketing down, seeping under collars, running under leggings, making spectacles blind.

Perhaps it is the practice, perhaps it is the mantra, the Beds become progressively easier to negotiate. Flat flags now between the rocks, balm to battered feet.

The rain splatters off the grocers' plastic bag peaked on the head of a middle-aged man in a suit.

34

Walk six times around the outside of the large Penitential Bed (which comprises St Patrick's Bed and that of Ss Davog and Molaise) while saying six *Our Fathers*, six *Hail Marys* and one *Creed*.

Kneel at the entrance to St Patrick's Bed (nearer the men's hostel) and say three *Our Fathers*, three *Hail Marys* and one *Creed*. Walk three times around the inside while repeating these prayers. Kneel at the Cross in the centre and say them again.

Kneel at the entrance to the Bed of Ss Davog and Molaise (nearer the water's edge) and say three *Our Fathers*, three *Hail Marys* and one *Creed*. Walk three times around the inside while repeating these prayers. Kneel at the Cross in the centre and say them again.

There is a kind of peace descending. The rounds and rounds of prayers and circling feet exclude the other pilgrims' sounds and rounds, the world reduced to feet and stones and prayers.

Go to the water's edge; stand, and say five *Our Fathers*, five *Hail Marys* and one *Creed*. Kneel and repeat these prayers.

The water's edge. The end is near.

The water's edge, a little slipway to the lake, pocked with slabs. The water mournful and stippled with the rain, pungent diesel-rainbowed at the edges.

Some step into the oily water, allowing it to lap above their ankles, relic of ancient times when exercises involved immersion.

Return to St Patrick's Cross; kneel, and say one *Our Father*, one *Hail Mary* and one *Creed*.

The puddled stones are almost soft, the fluted column almost warm, the Station nearly over...

Conclude the Station in the Basilica by saying five *Our Fathers*, five *Hail Marys* and one *Creed* for the Pope's intentions.

The blissful parquet flooring in the busy church is soft as down and just as welcome. The prayers fly...

But now they must be done again, every one.

And then when they are done, they must be done again...

The rain is just as cold again, the queue is twice as long...

At the end of one Station, a pilgrim has recited ninety-nine *Our Fathers,* one-hundred-and-sixty-two *Hail Marys,* seven *Glorias* and twenty-six *Creeds.*

Before leaving Lough Derg, a pilgrim must complete nine Stations.

This means he will have recited eight-hundred-and-ninety-one *Our Fathers,* one thousand, four-hundred-and-fifty-eight *Hail Marys,* sixty-three *Glorias* and two-hundred-and-thirty-four Creeds.

Plus several Rosaries and assorted *Our Fathers, Hail Marys, Creeds* and *Glorias* as trimmings to the other ceremonies on the island.

The priest gave me Hail Marys *for my penance this morning in confession — and I asked him could he not be a bit more original...!*

Male pilgrim

37

9.30 pm. Night Prayer and Benediction

The rain outside defeats the evening light, but fails to drown the steady hymns in the basilica which is bright with massive bracts of electric light:

Nearer my God to Thee;
Day is done, but Love unfailing;
Abide with me.

For those for whom the battle is won — the Pilgrims of the Second Day who go soon to sleep — the recitation of the *Canticle of Simeon*:

Save us, Lord, while we are awake; protect us while we sleep;
that we may keep watch with Christ, and rest with him in peace.
At last, all-powerful Master,
you give leave to your servant to go in peace, according to your
promise...

And then the old reliable from the incense days of school and from procession days for Corpus Christi or The May, *Tantum Ergo* for the Benediction.

The candle of the vigil, which was so tall, has grown stubby and is formally extinguished with a candle-snuffer. The drooping rows of pilgrims who have survived the ordeal watch avidly for its extinction. Most can no longer kneel, but support themselves on seat and elbows.

A young blonde girl, a Pilgrim of the Second Day, raises an exultant clenched-fist sign of victory over sleep and hunger, rain and wind and pain.

The First Day Pilgrims brace themselves, knowing that another candle will be brought and lit for them tonight. They watch in (holy) envy as the released souls head for the dormitories.

(And while the pilgrims pray inside, the squads of students flit like busy shadows round the open spaces near the shelters, sweeping up the butts of cigarettes.

"People who never smoke — the first thing they do when they get on the island is to go to the shop and buy a packet of cigarettes"
— Monsignor McSorley, prior of Lough Derg.)

10.15 pm. Introduction to Vigil

This is Holy Hour.

The great doors of the basilica are banged shut, shutting away the pilgrims for one full hour.

In older days, a low and narrow cave was closed for one full day and one full night.

And as in older days, when bishops were obliged to dissuade pilgrims intent on coming to Station Island, the priest in charge this night outlines the terrors of the night to come, the need for 'friendly elbows' in the ribs when fellow-sufferers lose the fight to sleep, the difficulty of concentration in the mental fog pre-dawn, the questions which will be asked as to why this chalice cannot pass.

He commemorates another 'Twalfth' in 1795, when a full boatload of pilgrims, ninety people in all, was lost in the lake, pulled under by vicious currents.

But when their bodies were scoured from the bed of the black lake, clutched in the hand of a woman from Derry, known only as 'Miss O'Donnell', was a small penal cross...

The little cross is echoed in the great cross over the altar of the basilica, a cross of hope, because on its base is commemorated the legend of the cock which crew when Peter had denied Christ for the third time. That ancient legend has it that on the day after Christ was crucified, the cock which crew was taken for the pot.

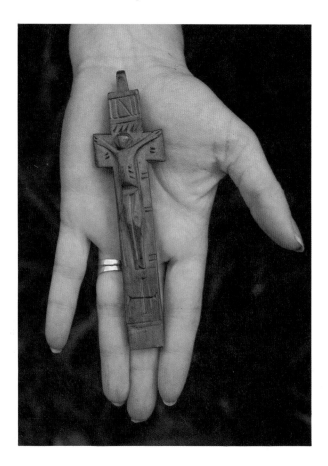

But on Easter Sunday, after Christ left the tomb, the cock which was in the roasting skillet was also given back its life and flew free, flapping its wings and singing praises... *Mac na hÓighe slán, Mac na hÓighe slán!*

The Virgin's Son is safe.

The priest commends the pilgrims to a mode of listening which will allow the Word of God to reach their hearts. Prayer is a two-way street.

The vigil candle, tall again, is lit, the priest withdraws and the pilgrims face the night alone.

The older pilgrims and repeaters settle down in contemplation. Conservation is the essence of the night, energy and concentration fed out slowly on filmy strings attached to dawn.

The younger ones with friends confer in nervous giggles. The struggle is at hand, the enemy as yet unsighted.

There is a Rosary which leads to midnight, a bridge from night to morning.

12.30 am. Fourth Station

"We don't want any broken legs. We don't want you to go to the water's edge and never be seen again..." the young priest (the jolly one) had said, as he listed out the 'do's and don'ts' for the night. "Although it might appear as though we don't have your welfare at heart, we do..."

And so the four Stations of the night are performed inside the basilica.

"Inside the basilica," starts the pilgrim at the lectern at 12.30 am... *"Our Father Who art in Heaven....*

"Standing at St Patrick's Cross... *Our Father Who art in Heaven...*

"Kneeling at St Brigid's Cross... *Our Father Who art in Heaven...*
"Walking around the outside... *Our Father Who art in Heaven...*

The brain is firing, the heart is firm, the feet move willingly around the church.

"Kneeling at the entrance to St Brigid's Bed... (*Our Father...*)
"Walking on the outside... (*Our Father...*)
"Walking on the inside... (*Our Father...*)

and then — the end in sight —

"Standing at the water's edge... (*Our Father...*)"

The leader's voice is strong, the pilgrims' voices stronger in response. They are confident in battle. They stand and walk and kneel, stand and walk and kneel and stand and walk in unison, rosaries in use, congregation abacus counting off *Our Fathers* and *Hail Marys* and *I Believes* in steady rhythmic pulses. The penitential beds had been a solitary test. The 'Inside Station' is an exercise in bonding, a wheeling unitary prayer from an army on the move.

When it is over, at 1.30, the pilgrims have a break. Some sit in contemplation, some rummage through their handbags or turn their sodden jackets on the makeshift hangers on the pews; some choose to walk outside, although the route is merely round and round the flagstones in the rain and wind; some scurry to the lakeside shelter for a ciggy and a chat.

"How do you feel now, Margaret?"
"Grand..."
"Tired yet?"
"Not a bit..."
"Looking forward to the kippers in the morning?"
"Yeah..."

At this time the buttressed night-shelter which stands on pillars in the waters of the lake, is fugged with smoke from cigarettes and gamy with the smell of dampish wool on human bodies. It is long and narrow, with seating back to back and strutted roof, a smaller version of the waiting-room for the Staten Island ferry.

Waystation on the route to heaven.

2.00 am. Fifth Station

A muted bell recalls the pilgrims to their Exercises.

Again the leader calls the prayers:

"Kneeling at St Patrick's Cross (*Our Father...*)
"Walking around the outside of the Basilica... (*Our Father...*)

Some younger ones begin to falter. It is 2.30 and they miss some standings and some kneelings but sit with staring eyes and barely moving lips. They rally towards the end, *Hail Mary, Holy Mary...*

The pilgrims shuffling round the floor are slow, the crowd is large; easier for some to shuffle up and down the kneelers in the pews, up and down, up and down, the rhythm suited to the individual:
Hail Mary, Holy Mary,
up and down, up and down,
walk for *I Believe*;

up and down, up and down
Hail Mary, Holy Mary,
stretch the arms, renounce the devil,
Hail Mary, Holy Mary;

Mesmeric...

The young priest (the serious one) was right when he advised a "giving in to the rhythm of the pilgrimage". The prayers lead, the body follows.

At the water's edge at last...

The break at 3.00 am is welcome. The wind at least has died, the rain is only spatting.

Again the shelter is blue with smoke. Pilgrims queue to drink the water from the little fountains on the wall outside. From springs below the lake, it seems as sweet as honey.

"How do you feel now, Margaret?" (the older woman is solicitous)
"I feel wrecked. I'm not going to make it..."
"You are, of course. Sure haven't you the half of it over you..."

The words are low but clearly audible. All around, the chat has died. The bluish fug from cigarettes is stronger now, more acrid to the dragging senses.

Some heads inside the church collapse on necks too weak to hold them. They raise themselves with difficulty with the bellcall to the Sixth Station.

3.30 am. Sixth Station

The difficulty now is that this is not the last. It is the last but one, but not the last.

Up and down, up and down, the muscles pull protesting, the eyes are hot, the cheeks are cold, the feet are almost numb.
Kneel and stand and walk
Kneel and stand and walk

And pray...

"You don't pray here with your lips, you pray with your whole body"
Monsignor McSorley

More and more, some bodies can no longer push. They sit and lean their heads on pews in front or on the shoulders of a neighbour. A young girl faints. Another staggers as she walks her last before she falls asleep. The Christian crowd which shuffles still around and past these suffering bodies is vastly charitable. Despite the early exhortations from the priest, no friendly elbows in the ribs. No censure.

You meet yourself. Is **that** your soul?

4.30 am...

The break is not a respite, not a chance for rest. This break
is where the battle peaks inside the church or in the shelter.
The darkness comes in wavy pillows.
It jerks at unsuspecting heads.
It cushions eyes.

It scrambles understanding. For when another pilgrim asks a
simple question, the words arrive in disarray.

"Do you know what time it is?", he asks (it seems)...

The words come in: *time Do knowyou itis what.*
And even on a second hearing: *know Doityou time whatis.*

But on the rims of hills around the lake outside, a pencil-gleam
of pearly light is rising to the sky. The rain has stopped and
pilgrims, grateful for the freezing air, can walk or watch the
coming dawn.

"There's only one more now, Margaret, you'll be grand."
"I know. I don't feel too bad now... I hope I can stay awake
for the Mass. That's the next worry..."
"Well don't worry about that. The Lord'll forgive you, I'm
sure, even if you don't manage. We'll look after each other,
OK?"

(There are still seventeen and a half hours to pass before sleep
is permitted.)

5.00 am. Seventh Station

The dawn has broken over Kinnagoe across the water and with it comes a second wind for pilgrims, a knowledge that the dreaded night is over. Although the flesh is weak and hurting, the spirit drives it on.

The sleepers wake and join the Station. A pilgrim with a dragging leg renews his efforts up and down his pew; the travelling woman with the brightly coloured stockings pulls and pushes her heavy bulk along her bench with one hand, praying her Rosary fervently with the other. The tired priest she helped around the penitential beds moves painfully around the floor.

Up and down the kneeler, up and down, *Hail Mary, Holy Mary,* one foot in front of the other, smooth wood under the arch (watch the split where one plank joins another) kneel, stand, *Hail Mary, Holy Mary,* curl the toes around the edges, feel the wood, feel the wood, *Hail Mary, Holy Mary,* pivot on the balls and turn around, *Hail Mary, Holy Mary* as the natural light begins to filter through the glory of the stained glass windows, kneel, stand, turn again, *Hail Mary,* one foot in front of the other, *Hail Mary,* push, push, *Hail Mary,* only St Patrick's Bed and Cross to go, *Hail Mary, Hail Mary,* At The Water's Edge...

Thank God.

Another break before the morning Mass.

The bodies now are casualties. Without the screen of moving, shuffling Station pilgrims, the basilica is a spent battlefield with littered corpses and discarded useless armour. Plastic macs adorn its doors, headscarves lie untidily in heaps along its seats, woollen scarves and coats are hung along its galleries, plastic **bags from Harrod's and Dunnes Stores line its walls.**

But a brilliant sun has risen high outside. It streams in, golden through the open doors, and like the Newgrange summer solstice, lights the tabernacle in the sanctuary.

"It's a beautiful morning, Mary, and we've the worst of it over, thank God."

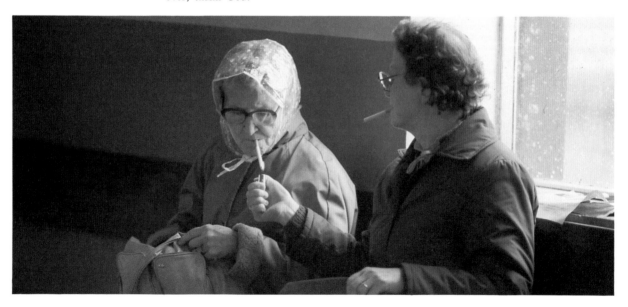

6.30 a.m. Morning Prayers and Mass

Early morning Mass for First Day Pilgrims is an endurance test of a different order. The Second Day Pilgrims arrive, scented, powdered and refreshed and add their cheerful body warmth to the pews. Comfort to succumb now. Softness all around. Who'd see?

And all around there are gentle sounds of even breathing and even snores...

But the energetic priest will not allow it. From the altar, he stretches out his energy for all to grasp.

Many fail to reach it and nod off.

The priest is not without a sense of humour: "Will all the people who are awake, please stand to pray!"

There is humour in Lough Derg, a special, prison, commune type of humour.

The cheapest bed and breakfast in Ireland
A place of spiritual hi-fibre
A holy health farm
A concentration camp of the soul
A place where only black-belt Christians need apply

The conversations in the mornings deal on sizzling rashers, runny eggs; on massive joints of roasted beef and mounds of mashed potatoes — as fasting pilgrims sip hot water laced with pepper or, freezing, hover on hotwater-pipes in the special room for drying clothes.

49

The Second Day is well advanced, time to look around.

On any given day during the ten-week season, there are usually four priests on Lough Derg, including the prior. There are three nuns, one of whom is a nurse, one an expert in domestic science. There are fifteen lay staff and five clerical students.

There are 640 beds in the new women's hostel and 340 in the men's. The basilica can accommodate 1200.

The area of the island was originally an acre, it is now just over four — the new building put on an acre.

The architect of the new building and of the new sanctuary is Joe Tracey. The marble altar and lectern are by Peter McTague. The tabernacle was sculpted by Patrick McElroy.

The number of pilgrims in any season at present is as high as 30,000.

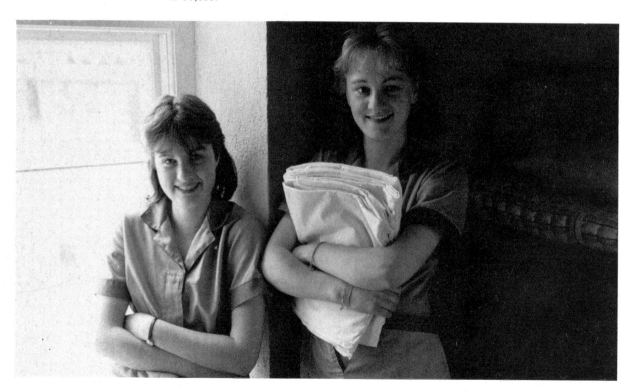

This pilgrimage today is largely middle-class...

"I don't quite know how to answer that question..." The Monsignor is standing at the door of the men's hostel. "I think that would be more a matter of tradition. The tradition was never there in some areas. A lot of the people who come here might have started for results of exams in secondary school or in university. There was a time when entire GAA teams might come here before or after games. The rugby teams used to come too and many individuals continued on afterwards. We would see, too, in the northern half of the country, that there was a tradition of coming here in certain families."

On the other hand the desperate come here too. "We still get a large number of people coming here who are out of work, praying for jobs, parents praying for their children to get work. That's part of the dimension of Lough Derg. The island is a barometer to the economic situation in the country too... during the Seventies when things were going well in the country, there was a drop off here, we were down to 17 or 18 thousand. There was a turn when the Pope came, but then when things started getting tough in the country, our numbers really went back up. When times are hard, people are inclined to pray — they're inclined to think 'if the Lord is above, maybe I should be getting in contact with him...' "

The Monsignor agrees that far greater numbers of women travel here proportionately to men although the equation is improving slightly: "When I started it was 4.1 to 1, now that's down to 3.8.

"All who come here come with something on their minds. The ministry here is different to when we are in the parishes, that is why we take care to be so visible, to be always around, so that people can approach us if they want to.

"And there is no rush, no-one's going anywhere, there is plenty of time... Confession here is not only a question of confessing your sins and getting absolution, there is the question of counselling — how are you, are you happy, is your marriage happy, how are things at work — and letting people talk and *listening*..."

But this can be a lonely place, particularly lonely if you are here without a group or a friend. The long night hours are longer without a friend. If your feet cannot make the extra inches to the holy water font, your friend will flip the holy drops against your face; if you feel you need a laugh between the Stations, your friend will tell you a joke; if the thousandth *Hail Mary* is utterly meaningless, a glance at your friend's face and an empathetic roll of eyes to heaven will give you heart for the thousandth and first...

You can kneel beside your friend when the priests disperse to their posts behind the altar-rails and the prie-dieux to hear the individual confessions of the barefoot, fasting, exhausted pilgrims. Together you can watch to see which priest to choose:

"Very often," says Monsignor McSorley, *"they make the choice from the way you speak to them in ordinary conversation when you meet them around the place — or maybe they identify with something you've said off the altar which strikes a chord in their lives.*

"The other thing would be that they can see the various priests' reaction to the different penitents coming up to them. A lot of people have problems, maybe they've gone off the rails and want to put things right, make a fresh start, and there is a lot of apprehension there normally — 'I wonder how the priest is going to react' — then they see that none of the priests are showing any temper.

"You'd have someone who says 'it's been so long since my last confession' — and you'd say, 'well, it must have taken a bit of courage to get that out' — and you're away..."

The organist plays long peaceful chords as priests reach out to touch the arms and heads of kneeling people — one even gives a hug; this ceremony of reconciliation is central to the pilgrimage — for some it is too difficult. Having waited for an hour or more, a young man rises quietly and leaves the church and does not come back.

"Some people come here five, six, even seven times before they finally get out what is on their minds," said the priest at Mass this morning.

The Eighth Station on the outside Beds and then the soul goes quiet in the long reaches of this Second Day. Structured thought is almost impossible in a brain parched for sleep.

The renewal of baptismal promises at noon. The devil is renounced and at bay.

This day is when the troubled, turbulent outside world seems very far away.

(*Prayer is a two-way street...*)

When friendships flower:

"I have two invitations already for holidays in Northern Ireland — two *separate* ones!"

(In older days it was the day when boys met girls and took them later for their wives...)

The brylcreemed gent with seamy face is walking round and round the outside of the basilica:

"Enforced boredom."

By the time he passes on his second round, he has thought better of 'enforced boredom': "I didn't mean that — say that I think it's 'instant satisfaction.' "

On the third round he reveals that he got into trouble in another country, thousands of miles away, "very very severe trouble, you cannot know how severe". He is here for the fifth time, having travelled the world, shouldering his burden of guilt and trouble and being assured by priests everywhere that he need not forever do penance. He seems not to have believed the priests.

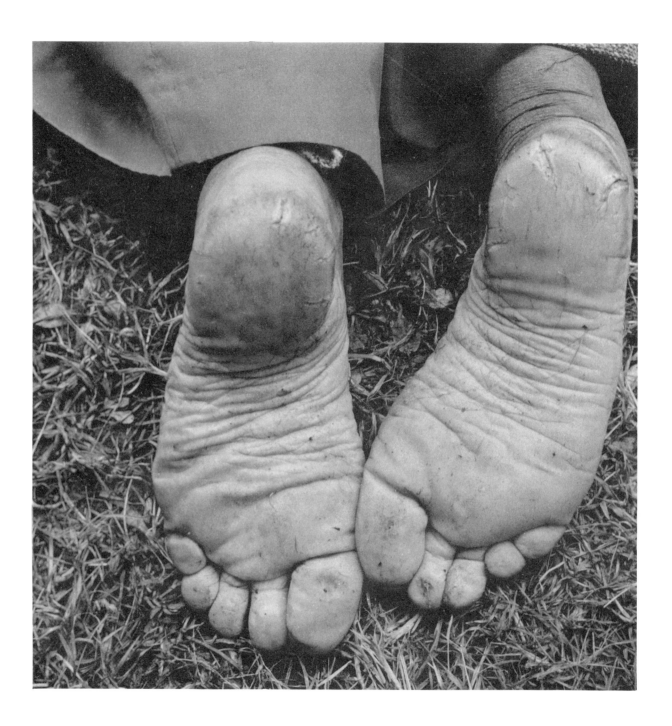

She has been here thirteen times. Some others point her out. Not for the frequency of her coming here, but for her feet. Her welted feet, sore and cut from the Beds, are worthy of note.

She is old and "on the disability for the mental". No Magdalen but Martha whose eyes are black with tiredness, who wears no marriage rings and whose lined and sore-pitted face shows only care and even malnutrition.

"I was slipping in the rain there on the Beds this morning and it wasn't really doing the Beds because I couldn't think of my prayers, but then I thought about it and I realised I *was* doing the right thing. I don't have to be perfect, I just have to do the best I can. It's not so much all the *Hail Marys* and the *Our Fathers*, it's the discipline of the whole thing on your body and your spirit. It's a complete break from your everyday life. It's a cut-off. I wouldn't feel my halo any bigger or anything like that, but I feel I need it. You're not 'great to do Lough Derg', if you're doing it for your own honour and glory, you're not doing it right at all. It just gives you time to think and to sort out a few things..." — telephonist.

59

The man from Cork has come for twenty-one of the last twenty-five years. He is not devout above the average, he says. His mother died when he was very young but before she died, she handed on a tradition, an example of Christianity that he cherishes.

He does not question overmuch in the areas which trouble many thinkers, the concepts of physical heaven and hell for instance. "As a practising Christian, I really don't examine that area very deeply. It's an area that I would be slightly afraid to examine in that I stand back from it and I lead an everyday Christian life, maybe leaving someone else to answer. It's an area that I personally find that if I get too deeply into, I get confused. And I don't wish to get into that state. I'm happy enough to accept what I am told."

That he does not question does not mean he is not a thoughtful man. "This whole area of sin — what it is, how it changes. Once it was a sin to eat meat on Fridays... it is simply easier to take the changes, take them as I get them."

He was inquisitive at first about Lough Derg and demanding: "imploring the Lord for the marks in the Leaving Cert", but then he developed an attachment to the place.

He has a lot of things in his life to be thankful for. Compared to the real sufferings of others, a few days' fasting and lack of sleep is nothing. The most rewarding thing is the personal one of achievement: "Normally you are observing other people, but in this situation, you are observing yourself. You have an opportunity to analyse yourself and balance your own personal books, asking yourself 'how am I living? How do I deal with myself, my family, my friends, my neighbours, my job?' You take a total look. It's a place where you get isolation and detachment, an opportunity to examine everything.

"It is quite unique in one way. It is so physically tough that the only path open is one of total honesty. You have to tell yourself the truth about yourself. You can get away with a lot of self-deception in your ordinary life, pretending you're asking yourself questions but getting answers that are not totally the truth. Why bother to come here and go through all of this if you are not going to face yourself?

"I think one has the right not to believe if it is square with one's conscience, in the same way as there is no point in my believing something if my conscience says otherwise.

"I had the experience, one time, of bringing a classmate in college with me to this place, who at the time was not a practising Christian and who, unfortunately, isn't yet... When we arrived in the basilica, he used some very strong language to me about the place. But at the end of the two days, he found it a very fulfilling exercise, insofar as he observed how other people lived and their values, as opposed to his own. He understood that their values were as valid as his own and that they wished to be allowed to continue with them.

"I think in the eyes of Holy God, there is no problem with that. The Gospels say that it is up to a person to live by the talents they are given. On the last day, we are told, everyone will be measured by how they have used those talents. I think if people lived by their conscience and did their best not to harm others in a deliberate way, then they have as much right to eternal salvation as any who have been practising rigorously."

The place abounds with kindness, especially on this Second, longest, toughest day:

"Oh look, those puir wee souls... with all tha' still ahaid of them this night..."

"But that was *you* last night..."

"Aye but tha's gone! It's like the snow upon the ground tha' once was white and noo is gone for ever..."

Alice Sherry and Grace McGuire, two friends, Pilgrims of the Second Day. A priest's housekeeper and a priest's helper, both from Glasgow, cheerful island of chat and laughter ("Wait 'til Fr Walshe hears aboot this! Don't show all ma wrinkles!") on the lakeward ramparts.

Alice is a first-timer.
"Actually I'd no notion of coming here — no thought of coming here at all. It was Gracie here who said she was away to Lough Derg and she said would I like to go...

(You rarely know why you are here at Lough Derg. But God knows.
— priest at the Holy Hour)

"I said 'aye'. I said to meself I want to do something in ma life. A really strenuous penance once in ma life for the benefits I've had. So I've come here as a thanksgiving and a penance."

Gracie: "Well you're cairtainly no' havin' a holiday!"

Alice: "At home you go to your own Masses, you go to your own services, but here it's entirely different.

"I dinna know. It's mebbe the place, it's mebbe th'atmosphere, you don't know — but there seems to be just that something. Soothing. Peaceful.

"It's no' easy, by no manner or means. When you go on tae the Beds you say 'I'll never make it, I'll never make it', you're trying to concentrate on the prayers you're saying — but I'm sure you miss out on some of them because you're so busy concentrating on where one foot goes in front of the other. I don't believe anyone goes on those Beds and says all those prayers — although they think them. But the spirit is there."

Gracie: "God knows you're trying."

Alice: "I feel more close to God now and as the time goes on this day I'm feeling more happy in maself."

Two other women, two softly-spoken women from Cavan, sit in the open concrete shelter facing the penitential beds. "We came last year and we said we'd do it three years in a row, we heard that that's what you're supposed to do..."

They actually came before, two years in a row, but then stopped, so now they are determined that next year they will make it the three.

And that may not be the end of it either. They might keep coming even after that but eyes on the immediate, achievable goal, they have not made any firm decision. "We don't know what's going to happen, really... at the moment it's just the three in a row."

One of them nearly never came back after the first time ever. "I thought it was outrageous. Desperate. It never stopped raining from the moment I first put my foot on the island. And at the end, I couldn't feel that bad and want to do it again, I thought. I made up my mind never, ever to come back.

"And here I am!" (she is still not too sure as to why) the discomfort is still desperate, "the queue's a terror", and look at that rain...

"It's a real Lough Derg day."

The good-looking lanky fellow, Kevin Owens, a student from Downpatrick, has heard about the three-times-in-a-row tradition. "If you come once you have to come three times, isn't that the way?" He sits on the grass beside the queue, nursing a toe he thinks he may have sprained. It is his first time. "I was told it wouldn't be too hard on me because it was my first time. I was told it would be a novelty..."

But last night was a killer altogether — try as he might, he could not stay awake for the Seventh Station, the one which spans the dawn.

Now he keeps himself going with the challenge of the whole thing. "I'm up there on them Beds and I'm falling and stumbling and there's old people flying around there like they have wings. It's unbelievable!"

(Kevin's youthful faith and stamina is not going to be put to shame by greater faith of older people...)

But he is very very hungry. He ate twenty-five rounds of the toast, but it made no difference. "Well, they're only half-slices, you know! And them wee biscuits are not nice..." He had them, though, "anything tastes nice when you're starving... I had their soup too — it's just lukewarm water with salt and pepper in it!" There was so much pepper in it that his lips were on fire...

He had also hoped, sneakily, that the talent might have been good. Lots of girls came to Lough Derg, he knew. But he hit a lean patch. Disappointed in that too, he was. "The talent is wicked, mostly old ladies and nuns!"

His granny used to tell him about this place but the picture in his imagination was nothing like the reality. "She'd tell me you'd walk in your bare feet on stones, but I had no idea that they were going to be like *that*..." — he points to the punishing stone circles rising towards the bell-tower, jagged steps on a tortuous medieval staircase.

On the other hand, he finds the sum of the experience spiritually rewarding. "It's out here on its own, isn't it, you even have to come out on a boat to it. If it wasn't an island, if it was linked to the land, it wouldn't be the same — you've to travel in a boat, you've to walk in your bare feet just like people for thousands of years. You think about that when you're on those stones... that all helps you to pray..."

And in the anteroom of the men's hostel, the shoeless men in brown suits over old pullovers sit beside the young white-faced boys. They rest between their Exercises, puffing pipes and watching the smoke rise behind the copper boiler, dispenser of the famous 'Lough Derg soup' .

The big thing about this place is that everyone who comes has a good reason for coming and they would be very slow to articulate it. That's what we always tell reporters.

Monsignor McSorley

"I'm here because I'll be running out of Lough Dergs," says a man, 74, whose fifth time this is and who started coming only five years ago at the age of 69.

"Maybe I come to say thanks to the Man Above and maybe I come so that he'll keep giving it to me," says another.

And the gentle man from Monaghan wears a spruce white collar and tie. He came first forty-three years ago in 1945. He came a few times. And then he got married so he missed the years in between. But he always knew he'd come back.

"I think it does you a lot of good in every way, physically as well as every other way. I always feel my body clean as well as my soul."

71

There are teachers here whose faces — and perhaps fists — have inspired terror through the generations. Sockless, shoeless, their tired pale faces are suddenly ordinary, bereft of power.

There are doctors and consultants, stripped of mystery and aloofness; pillars of industry and the breweries; county managers and restaurateurs.

And in the women's hostel are consultants' and accountants' wives whose lambent style runs writ in Dublin 4, who wear designer labels, but who are no more protected from the rain than those who paid £3 for plastic macs with hoods.

''You would be absolutely amazed at the prominent men who come here. And when the men take it up, they are much more compulsive than the women. They start to come all the time...''

— woman, probably prominent herself in Certain Circles.

The Duke of Norfolk came and so did 19-year-old Michael Dooley from the parish of Mount Argus in Dublin 6. He lives in Sundrive and is unemployed although he has worked for Anco and for Rehab a little bit. Michael thinks that Lough Derg is truly the most wonderful experience of his life. He has always felt close to God, a true *duine le Dia*, and he loves Our Lady very very much. And although his stomach is empty and growling, he knows you can't die from fasting. "It's good for us. God likes us to do this."

Michael is utterly cheerful and sunnily appreciative of all that Lough Derg can give. "Once every twenty-four hours, you get lovely toast and lovely tea. It's a meal anyway, it's better than nothing. You have a nurse at night to look after you and this lovely church, and you get to sleep in lovely beds.

"And four Masses in three days, that's really great..."

Michael will certainly, "certainly" (he cannot say it too often "*certainly*") come here again.

There are young girls with chipped red polish on their stubbed toes and tired mothers of eleven whose varicosed feet show legacies of every pregnancy.

And county hurlers who once got fifty-six stitches in their skulls.

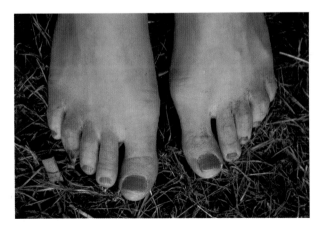

And even a boatload of Vietnamese, people who have travelled
with their priest from Birmingham...

A young freckled boy, Seamus O'Donnell from Tyrone, too young for penance, grey with fatigue but determined not to show it, whizzes around the Stations, round and round, passing out the feeble and the arthritic: ''Excuse me, excuse me', interrupting his *Hail Marys*, lashing the air with his beads, having an adventure, completing a tough task, something to bring back to school.

''The last two years he's been crying every time I came and was leaving him behind, he got it tough last night, but he has youth on his side,'' says Seamus' Dad.

Another boy from Cornwall, 15, bewildered: ''Me Mum and sister came so I came too. It's a different experience...'' (then, considering) ''I'm not very religious at home — only *pretty* religious...

''I haven't worked out yet what it means, but (with 15-year-old generosity) I *think* it's going to do me a lot of good.''

75

██ ██

John Prior, a member of the Irish Christian Brothers from New York, is based in a tiny mission house in the Andes of Peru. A strongly-built, bearded man, he is wet, cold ''and frustrated — because walking around those circles, each time is just as bad as the other'' — and appears to be shell-shocked by Lough Derg.

''What is it? An experience? A happening? A challenge? I guess it's all of that...''

He agrees that, coming towards nightfall on the Second Day, he is at the nadir of pain and discomfort. ''I don't know what it's doing for me spiritually. I am very glad I came — but I think I'll be very glad when I finish! I think I feel the same way I did when I first went skiing, when I was freezing and falling all the time. The best time then was when I took my boots off in the evenings... I guess I'll have to wait for the totality of this experience to know what it means.''

At the present moment, he feels closer to God in one way and not in another. ''I can't say prayers quickly as you have to do here — and fighting against the stones, it's very hard to say prayers. But I know it's a human experience of spirituality. Other religions have the whirling dervish going round and round. Buddhist monks and Hindu monks have the constant repetition until they begin to enter a whole new state. So I think that for humans to express ourselves to God in human ways, many things should be common between the Hindus and the Buddhists and ourselves.''

He struggles to find this commonality in Lough Derg, but stops short at the barrier of the pilgrimage's unique changelessness: ''In Peru you have long walks into the desert, up the high mountains, processions which take all day. But there is always the feeling there that the Church is *moving...*" In Lough Derg, the Church is reaching backwards to an ancient tradition, opening up the past with rites which have not changed for 1500 years.

John Prior's mother was born in Tyrone. His memory lifted a flimsy curtain, while he was actually on the Beds, and he remembered that he had known about Lough Derg all along. "I didn't expect to be here at all. I had heard some people commenting on the existence of Lough Derg and I understood from them that if you want to touch some part of the soul of the Celt, you really had to come here. But while I was doing the rounds, it came to me. I remembered my mother telling me she 'did' Lough Derg. It's really something extraordinary to me to realise that I am walking in my bare feet on the very stones that my mother walked in her bare feet..."

In Peru, the old religious rituals and mass processions have been preserved despite initial objections by the young priests of 'liberation theology' — "they realised that if they were to identify with the people, then they had to understand that this is what the people feel." Ireland's traditional Christianity is penitential in nature and, therefore, Lough Derg is a true expression of the Celtic Catholic.

"I think the Celt had a faith which was very natural, based on nature, close to the streams and rivers of the earth. So for them to do penance, it would have to be physical and close to nature too. It's extraordinary — it's hard for me to believe that those rings, those Beds, are the ones that people circled a thousand years ago."

He is fascinated to hear that a woman came for the second time in the same season, because on her last visit the sun was shining and she felt she had not done it properly...

"My God!"

He is equally fascinated at Lough Derg's repeat business. "Somebody told me that sixty to seventy per cent of the people here have done it before..."

He cannot resist logic and begins to work out the attraction: "There is an American expression among the athletes — 'no pain no gain'. Maybe that's it!"

Despite his misery, he loves the other half of the Celtic soul — the part which grants immediate fellowship and allows laughter in the refectory over the miserable collations. "There's a tremendous amount of support from other people. Other people are doing exactly the same as you are, around and around — and it's just as hard for them. They take just a ten or fifteen-minute break and you hear them laughing and chatting over that black tea and then they come back out here and slug it out again... it's just amazing..."

His transatlantic upbringing has not prepared him for the lack of commercialism about the shrine. "If you'll pardon me for saying so, this place is way out in the middle of nowhere. Yet you have people coming all the time. I haven't seen advertisements for Lough Derg. No-one gets a pin, *I Did Lough Derg*, no-one gets tee-shirts, no credits, yet it appears people return..."

He is unclear as to whether God requires this sort of penance, or if penance is something which is felt to be endemically necessary by an emotional race which has its dark sides and does not trust its own joy: "Does God want this? I think people come away from this experience knowing themselves a little better, loving mankind a little better. I would tend to think, though, that Lough Derg would attract naturally good people. I also think, however, there is something to the whole idea of the Irishman anticipating something dreadful happening if things are going too well and he's happy."

The pilgrim called John has sinned grievously in his past life. He has drunk alcohol to excess. He has raped a woman.

"I was bad until Christ came into my life. I was evil. I was like an animal. I did nothing to help myself and then one day I accepted Christ."

"You're not really here on your own accord. It's an invitation from Christ to come here. It's not everyone who comes here. It's not everyone who's *invited*."

"Can you eat? You'll be OK if you can eat."

The refrain is heard over and over.

The eating, once on each of the three days, is of dry toast or a small chewy oatcake. The drinking is of black tea or black coffee, sugar permissible.

A woman cannot eat at all, she has the dry retches. "I cannot eat," she says. "I cannot stand the smell of food. The minute I smell that toast, it gives me the dry heaves."

The experience is common, but unwise.

"Some of them come here and don't eat or drink at all, that's really stupid."

Annie McGrath, the night nurse,
who has to deal with the consequences.

The Meal. To be taken once a day during the pilgrimage.

The refectory is bright and new, with windows along both sides and furnished with long trestle tables and benches. There is no ligging or lagging behind. A Sister Frances hooshes everyone in together, packing them tightly at the tables, bright-eyed boys from Derry beside gentle women from Meath. It is an efficient operation with the helpers scurrying in and out of the kitchen carrying huge pots of tea and coffee and plates of soft dry toast, piled high.

An unfortunate child, about 17, sits miserably beside his mother. He had sat in with the rest and asked the worker, when she came, for "just a cup of tea".

The tea was poured and he was asked, by way of conversation, if he was not going to eat anything.

"No," he says, "I'm not. You see, I had my meal earlier. I just want a cup of tea now —"

"You'll not have a cup of tea — that's your lot for the day!" says the helper pertly... then those around him explain gently that under the rules of the Exercises, she is right.

For the remainder of his mother's meal, the poor boy sits, drooping miserably over the cooling cup of tea, while all around him people chew and chatter.

"I cregged me toe something shockin'. I knew I had to creg it sooner or later — it wouldn't be Lough Derg if I didn't!"

— young girl hobbling.

The Dublin woman, Rose Fay, mother of eleven, who is here with her friends from Kimmage, Rosaleen Clegg and Bernie Winters, could never be persuaded to go to the seaside for fear that she might be expected to take off her shoes and paddle.

When Rose was a child, her own mother used to have to have slippers ready at the side of the bath because she could not bear the sensation of any surface except footwear under her bare soles.

"And when I was coming up here yesterday, the young one was shouting after me, 'Mammy, d'ya want your slippers?' I've never been in my bare feet since the day I was born. That's as true as God and me the age I am...!"

Now here she is, barefoot, eight Stations over her, happy as Larry.

Now she'll be able to go to the seaside and all.

A little miracle.

John Halloran, a farmer from Navan who farmed a Land Commission farm of thirty-five acres all his life, is here for the first time, although he wanted to come for forty years and might even come back again next week. "I'm retired now and have little to do."

He sits upright as a ramrod on the hard wooden bench in the day/night shelter, his collar stiff, his tie correctly knotted, his cap firmly in place. Beside him are some of the women from his parish.

At home he lives alone. "I miss my wife very much." His wife died four years ago. He thinks about her and prays for her all the time. He passes the day by going to Mass in the morning and then cooking himself a breakfast and then doing the little jobs in the house. He never drank and so he does not go down to the pub, but the television is good company at night.

Stephen Lynskey, 17, from outside Scotstown, buys Seán
Mulligan, 14, from the same townland, a present from the
shop — a Padre Pio medal. The medal is on a chain.

Seán Mulligan sits on the bench seat outside the shop, holding
the shiny golden chain between his fingers, loving it very much.
His eyes are glittering with fatigue but he denies strenuously
that he is tired.

Conversations under the Loggia, the graceful pillared porches framing the entrances to the basilica:

"The worst of all, I find, is to go on those Beds on the third morning, when the muscles are all relaxed after the good night's sleep. 'Tis a killer altogether..."

"Ah no, the killer for me is the queue. When you're going round and round and the praying is coming automatically, you get into the rhythm of it all. And then you have to stop and stand in that frigging queue. Sometimes you have to stand in the wind and the rain for an hour and a half..."

"I dunno what it gives me — peace of mind, I suppose — I keep coming anyway... what about you?"

"I brought a fella here one time and he didn't believe all that strongly. But he's changed dramatically since. It really did the trick on him..."

(Pause, while the men stare off into the distance, at the nails of rain being driven into the pools and puddles.)

"What time is it now? What's next? Rashers, is it?"

"Why did I come here? I came here to get this jumper done!"

– Derry girl knitting under colonnade of new building.

"It's not the same", the woman says in disapproval as she sits among the wet-wool smells of drying clothes in the brand-new, heated 'drying-room'. "Look at *this* for instance — a place to dry your clothes! And there are flagstones all around the basilica. That is luxury.

"*Coffee* now as well as tea!" That is luxury —

"They used to empty gravel on the penitential beds to make them worse, scattering it from a wheelbarrow..."

As she sat beside the warming pipes, the woman felt the loss of gravel.

She mourned the passing of the old women's hostel with its concave sleeping pallets and special depths of decaying discomfort.

"It's not the same. It's lost something. Before, when you left, you felt you'd really *done* something..."

"Scattering gravel on the Beds? That's not true at all. There are people who think I spend my time in the winter going out with a chisel on those Beds, sharpening the stones!"
Monsignor McSorley, prior of Lough Derg

"God, it's not the same at all. I saw a boy kissing a girl last night in the night-shelter. In the old days, girls were not allowed to wear jeans or short-sleeved blouses. And if the old Monsignor found a romance book on the island, there'd be a big search and the owner'd be thrown off...!"

"In the old days, you'd see people, boys and girls going around, linking, well that was definitely frowned upon. Nowadays you accept the fact that people have feelings and faith and since I came here I don't think anyone's been sent off. But the rules are still the rules and that doesn't mean people haven't left. For instance, if you saw anyone who just wasn't doing the pilgrimage, not doing what they were supposed to be doing, if they were eating, or anything like that, I'd take them aside for a talk and I'd point out to them that this isn't the sort of place where you just come on to do your own thing. And if they still persisted, I'd suggest that maybe they'd be better off going to some other place, a retreat house or something like that, where they'd have peace and quiet. You achieve the same thing quietly but in a different way."

Monsignor McSorley, prior of Lough Derg

And sure, with all the young "lovely" priests and the friendly Monsignor, it's a holiday camp nowadays, practically, a Butlins for the soul, not like the old days when the old Monsignor would prod with sticks ("and none too gently either") at the luckless who had nodded off; or, at the 6.30 morning Mass, "would let a roar out of him off the altar that'd wake the dead".

Now the announcements are all gentle admonition:
"Do your best, we know it's hard but this is very important."

(It's not the same at all.)

"The penances are exactly the same," says Monsignor McSorley.

"Years ago the staff here were more abrupt and the regulations were given, 'you do' or 'you don't'. Today, you'd meet someone in the course of a day and they'd tell you that by mistake they took their breakfast this morning — well, years ago, they'd have been thrown off the island. You don't do that to people any more. We don't shout at people any more. You wouldn't get away with that anyway — the people used to take that — they wouldn't take it now.

(And as for being poked with sticks, adds the Monsignor, you might have gently touched with your toe someone who was sleeping — and this gets translated in the re-telling to a mighty kick, the strength of which grows with each narration.)

Three married men sitting on a wall. They are initially reluctant to talk.

"I was dragged here," says one, whose third time it is. At least he was dragged the first time "and then I kept looking back when I was leaving the island...so here I am again!" (There is a superstition that those who look back at the island from the boat when leaving will always return.)

"Actually, we'd nothing else on this weekend — much," says another. "We knew it was going to be wet, too wet for golf. So we looked up the Bord Fáilte Guide..."

They become serious: "God's good, I suppose. I suppose that's why we came. We had to give something back..."

"You have to have a reason to do it for yourself. You need a reason to come on the island in the first place..." says the first.

"I'll tell you exactly why I'm here," says the second. "About three years ago, I had a financial problem. And I had tried everything else and this was a last resort. The problem hasn't resolved itself, but I'm kind of afraid to stop coming in case it gets worse. In any event it's three days during which you can think of nothing else except being here. You don't have time to think about your problems."

"I always have a reason for coming, either thanking or asking..." says the third. "The original reason I came was for my Dad. He wasn't that great in health and I wanted him to die with a priest. Two months after I came back from having done it (Lough Derg) he died. I was there and I managed to get him a priest. It was a good starter. And now it's difficult to break."

"It's a nearness to God, a closeness I suppose. You're saying that you're thinking of Him as well as Him thinking of you. It's a trade-off."

"Lough Derg? It's a bit like having a baby. After you get home you forget how bad it was and like an eejit, you come again." — pilgrim on the throes of the Second Day doldrums.

"Let me in from them flies or they'll eat me!" — pilgrim on coming into dayroom.

As if the Beds, the Stations, sore feet, the steely rods of rain, the fasting and the joust with sleep were not enough, the Lord has yet another test for pilgrims. He infests Lough Derg with plagues of biting midges...

So many midges that beside the rosaries and raincoats, the postcards, stamps, the holy pictures and the Happy Death Crosses (£3) the little shop on the island sells anti-midge cream called DUSK.

It is at dusk that they arrive. They rise from the water and swarm in numbers which to their victims seem like trillions. When you are tired, wet and hungry, their prickling attack is a Lough Derg reminder that the demons which tormented the English Knight Owain 841 years ago are not far away.

According to the legend which swept Europe in the twelfth century (and which is commemorated on the sculpted tabernacle in the new sanctuary of the basilica) the Knight Owain travelled to Lough Derg on penitential pilgrimage, probably in 1147. At that time, the pilgrimage lasted fifteen days and the fasting pilgrim was locked by the prior of the island into a cave, then believed to be the entrance to the other world, for twenty-four hours. Owain was locked in as was customary and was plagued by a succession of demons who tortured him with visions of hell but also of paradise.

This cave, centrepiece of the pilgrimage for centuries, was shut up by order of Pope Alexander VI in 1497 because of an allegation of simony, was opened again by Pope Pius III in 1503, was closed again by order of the ruling English Government in 1632 (being referred to in dispatches as a *poor beggarly hole*), was excavated again during the reign of the Catholic James II but was sealed off finally in 1780 by order of Lough Derg's prior, because the numbers of pilgrims had grown so great. Its site is thought to be under the present belltower, very close to the ancient Beds which are actually the remains of the cells constructed by medieval monks and on which modern pilgrims make their penance.

It has been said that the "strange pull" of Lough Derg, referred to almost unanimously by pilgrims who repeat their journey, is an answer to the call of blood. Penance is a natural part of religion to the Celt to whom solitude, repetitive prayer, vigil, fasting and physical endurance were the indispensable tools for the construction of spirituality. To the Celt, there is no purification without struggle. At one early stage in the history of the Irish Christian church, Ireland had three Lents — one before Christmas, one before Easter and the third after Pentecost.

Christ, it is said, fled to the solitude and harshness of the desert to struggle with his demons. In a wet and boggy country, the Celt fled to the solitude and harshness of the mountains or to Lough Derg.

In Ireland, penitential pilgrimage has been handed down, intact, since St Patrick brought Christianity here in 432. And from the early days of Christianity, fasting was a common spiritual exercise although there were two types of fasting, 'profitable' and 'unprofitable'. The 'unprofitable' type seems to have been adapted from paganism by Christianity for its own use in Ireland, as were pilgrimages, wakes, patterns and the sacredness of certain wells. While 'unprofitably' fasting, one person 'fasted against' another in competitive asceticism, almost as a curse. Patrick himself is said to have fasted 'against' King Laoire, whose son died, it is claimed, as a result. 'Profitable' fasting, on the other hand, was thought to be very beneficial to the soul and was undertaken in addition to the obligatory periods of fasting in the Christian calendar.

The modern pilgrimage to Lough Derg may not be as severe as it was 1200 years ago, but the pilgrims are encouraged to be hard on themselves. In that spirit, blankets or rugs (to ward off the cold of the night) are not allowed and — an instruction given in addresses from the altar of the basilica — leg-warmers are discouraged because they might slip (or be slipped) down over the ankles to give comfort to cold tired feet.

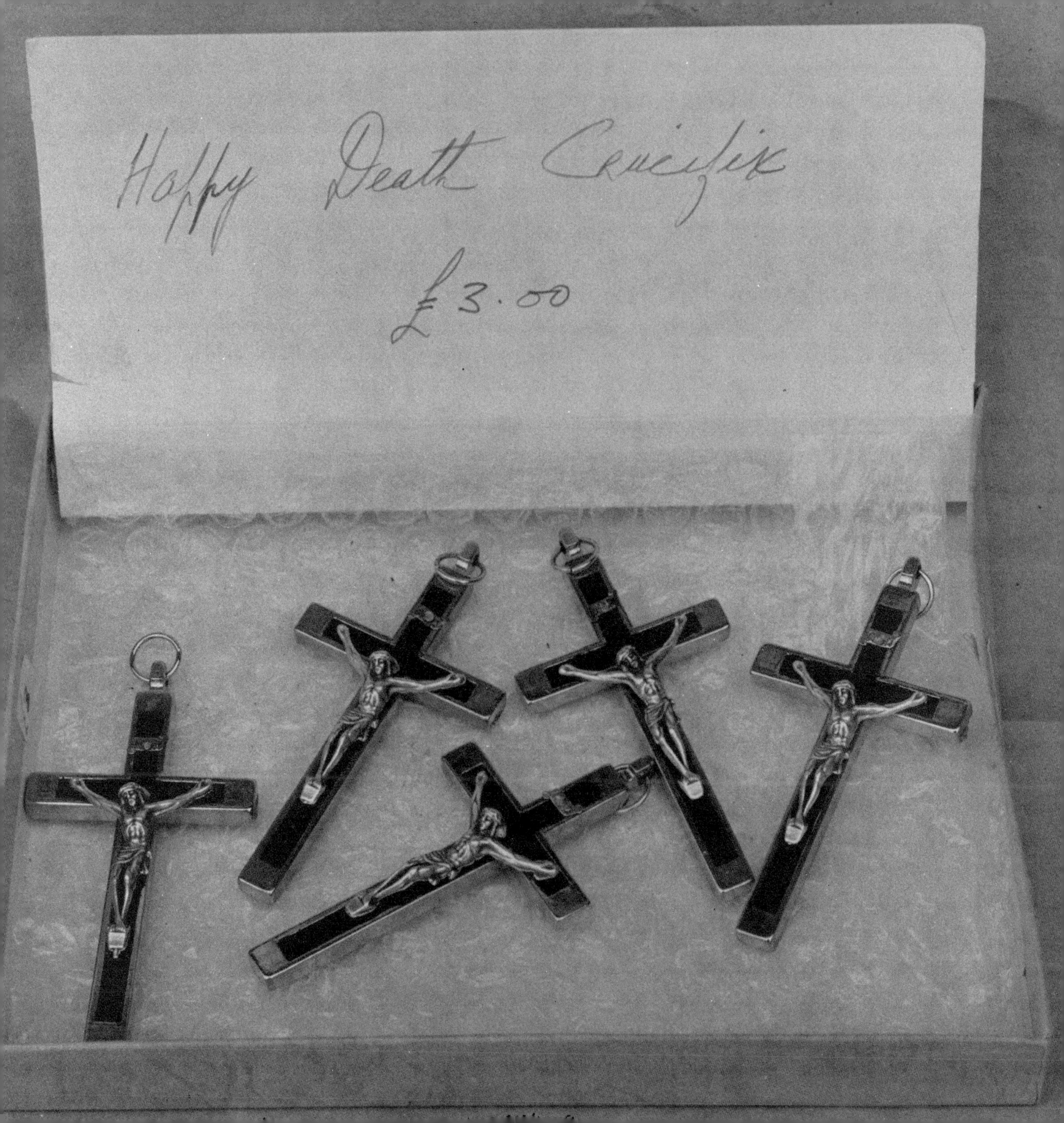
Happy Death Crucifix
£3.00

"Relief is at hand."

> — priest placing comforting arm around shoulders of pilgrim who is faltering, but who is entering the basilica for the night prayers and is therefore approaching the end of his vigil and the blessedness of sleep.

puRGaᴅóiR pÁᴅRaiG   st. patRick's puRGatoRy
loċ ᴅeaRG   louGh ᴅeRG
paite Gaḃa   pettiGo
co. tÍR ċonaill   co. ᴅoneGal

<u>LOUGH DERG MAXIMS</u>

I. Act always so as to maximise confusion and minimise comfort.

2. Act always so as to discriminate, interrogate and fustrate.

3. For every action there is an equal and equally negative reaction.

4. If the Organist requires an opion the Cantor will give it.

5. If at first you don't suceed your employment will be terminated.

6. Limitations of time and space are not acceptable as excuses.

7. If you wait around long enough, someone les qualified will end up doing

   your job for you.

8. Confessional Queing Practise. The **fir**st shall be last and the last firs

9. The Pilgrim is always wrong.

I0. If in doubt, bluff.

II. Pilgrims are to be heard and seen, but not listened to.

I2. Staff are not to feed the pilgrims.

I3. The amount of embarassment to be caused is directly proportional to the

    lateness of arrival for a liturgical function.

I4. Wherever three shall gather in my name a fourth will be talked about.

The outside lanterns on the lakeward ramparts click on gently,
timed to meet the dusk. From far away behind the coloured
windows, sound the strains of women singing:
Hail Queen of Heav'n the ocean star...
Be still and know that I am God.
The rain has stopped, the wind has dropped to nothing, the
sky has lifted to reveal a single evening star.
The silent bats come out in pairs and skim the surface of the
flattened water. The Second, longest day is nearly over.

And then there was the woman who gave out yards when
the lights were turned out in the dormitory and everyone else
was already snoring. She still had to put in her rollers...

The Third Day

Woman in headscarf, hands on hips, having just emerged from the dormitory on the morning of her Third Day:

"It can't be raining AGAIN!"

But it is. It is the Third Day and the sharp air is cold with blowing rain as usual. The pilgrims who have been up all night circle wearily outside the basilica. The seagulls scream from Saints' Island across the choppy water. Two wagtails chase one another in and out of the cloistered walk. The pages of a sodden *Financial Times*, three days old and discarded in the cloister by some pilgrim, are flicked by the fitful wind. 'PRAYERS FAIL TO EASE PLIGHT OF THE CORNBELT' is the newspaper's uppermost headline, referring to the drought in the USA...

Christ is reported to have said the following:

And when you fast, do not look dismal, like the hypocrites... anoint your head and wash your face, that your fasting may not be seen by men but by your heavenly father who sees in secret.

And the other side of Celtic Lough Derg is the upswing on the last day, the day when the end of the penance is in sight.

The young student helper has observed this: "You have to watch out for them in the morning after Mass on their last day. They have only one Station left to do and it's like the Naas dual carriageway between the basilica and the Beds in the rush to get on. They're fantastic on that last morning, swinging around the crosses and everything..."

While they must observe their fast until midnight, pilgrims are permitted, on the last day of their pilgrimage, to drink as many minerals as they want once they are off the island.

And they do.

The homegoing buses and cars pull in convoy into the town of Pettigo, where the residents are waiting with stalls laid out on the streets. The pilgrims load up on litres and pints and six-packs of minerals. They can also buy souvenir sticks of rock (*'A present from Lough Derg'*) or similarly annotated toy gnomes.

Back on the bus to Dublin a young girl draws long and deep through her straw on her large bottle of ice-cream flavoured soda: ''God, it's like a party,'' she says.

Nicky or maybe Nikki and her friend Patrina, are leaving today. Slickers and sleek hair, teacher and doctor, fiancées both, with marriage in very near prospect, next week, next month, "doing it for a happy and a holy marriage".

Patrina: "I do very very little really, normally. You know the way you do…"

Nicky or is it Nikki: "You know the way it's a cushy life in Dublin."

For each, each Station for a different intention ("this is the way you do it"). One for Mam and Dad. One for a sister doing exams. One for a granny who is very sick. One for a sick aunt.

One fiancé, Richard, came once, but took one look. Off the wall. Out to lunch. Ate, slept. Broke the rigid rules.

But when he went back to the mainland and the car, the clutch was gone. £220 sterling to have it fixed. Two days in Pettigo waiting for the parts.

Enough said…

In 1834, in *A Journey Throughout Ireland*, the author, Henry D Inglis, noted snidely:

...when the ferry discharged 'those whose penances were concluded' that they did not 'generally exhibit in their appearance and countenances, that expression of satisfaction which might be expected amongst those who had just abridged by some thousands of years, the term of their purgatory'.

A quick sample of quotations from departing pilgrims in 1988 demonstrates how blinkered that author was.

There is lightness:
"I feel great."
"Terrific."
"Can't describe it really. I really feel as if I've done something."
"The whole idea of Lough Derg is a new beginning. It's a cleansing. The sins of your past life are gone and forgiven. Each time I come here I feel clean."

Relief:
"...oh the shoes, isn't it great to get back on the shoes?"

Compassion (on observing new arrivals):
"... ahh! the poor creatures, they still have it all in front of them..."

Humour:
"Don't look back, Maura, for God's sake don't look back. You don't want to have us back here next year!"

And even superstition (as people throw money into the clear shallow water at the jetty):
"Why are you throwing in money?"
"I don't know — doesn't everybody?"
or:
"There's going to be another boating tragedy you know, like the one in 1795. It's going to happen when a nun and a red-haired woman get into the same boat..."

The Monsignor personally hands everyone down into the big grey leaving boats.

Thank you very much, Monsignor,
Thank you very much, Monsignor...

And then, when everyone is tightly packed, with handbags stowed and hoods severely tightened against the whipping wind, the boatman starts the engine.

A hymn is started, a few thin voices rising feebly in the rain, mostly women's: 'Hail, Glorious St Patrick'. (To please the Monsignor, do you see.)

Do not look back. The island with its circling pilgrims floats away.